WAR IN AFGHANISTAN AND IRAQ

Janet Souter and Gerry Souter

WHERE IS AFGHANISTAN?

Afghanistan is a country of mountains and deserts, on the continent of Asia.

Twenty-nine million people live in the country. Its capital is Kabul, and the other main cities are Kandahar, Herat, and Jalalabad.

In summer, temperatures can reach 120° F (49° C) in desert regions, and it can be very windy, with lots of sandstorms. Winter in the mountains is freezing, with heavy snow.

AFGHANISTAN IN THE WORLD

UZBEKISTAN

TURKMENISTAN

IRAN

PAKISTAN

Feyzabad

Mazar-e Sharif • Qonduz

Sheberghan • Kholm • Taloqan
Baghlan

Sar-e Pol

Meymaneh • Pol-e Khomri

Qaleh-ye Now

Bamian • Chariker

Herat

KABUL

AFGHANISTAN

Jalalabad

Gardez

Ghazni

Khowst

Farah

Delaram

Qalat

Kandahar

Zaranj • Lashkar Gah

N W E S

KEY
- Lowlands
- Hills
- Mountains

CANADA • UNITED KINGDOM • RUSSIA
UNITED STATES • CHINA
United States
SAHARA
BRAZIL
Afghanistan
AUSTRALIA

This old palace in Kabul was heavily damaged during the civil war in 1992.

AFGHAN CONFLICT

There are many different tribal groups in Afghanistan, and they sometimes fight among themselves. The country has suffered through several civil wars (fighting between groups within a country).

A group called the Taliban ruled in the 1990s and is now trying to retake the government of the country. Military forces from the United States and other countries are fighting to keep them from returning to power.

➡ What religion do Afghans follow?

Most Afghans are Muslims, which means they follow the religion of Islam. They pray five times a day in the direction of the Holy Islamic city of Mecca in Saudi Arabia.

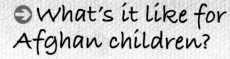

Muslim men pray in the direction of Mecca outside a mosque.

➡ What's it like for Afghan children?

Forty-three percent of Afghan people are children under fourteen. Many go to school, but many also work from an early age. In spite of all the hardship in their war-torn country, they play whenever they can. For instance, kite-flying is one of the most popular pastimes for Afghan children.

An Afghan child flies a kite on a hill above Kabul.

Many Afghans live in the valleys below snow-capped mountains.

 LIFE IN AFGHANISTAN

Life in Cities

In Afghan cities people work in shops and street markets, or in industrial jobs such as brick-making. Afghanistan is one of the poorest countries in the world, with an average yearly income per person of just $370.

Life in Villages

In the countryside, people live in villages. Eighty five percent of Afghans make a living by farming, growing crops, and keeping animals. The best farmland is in the country's fertile mountain valleys.

WHY DID THE WAR START?

On September 11, 2001, members of al-Qaeda, an Arab terrorist group, hijacked four planes.

They crashed two into the World Trade Center in New York and another into the Pentagon in Virginia. A fourth plane crashed in Pennsylvania. The terrorists were supported by the Taliban, who ruled Afghanistan in the 1990s, and allowed al-Qaeda to hide out in the country.

Al-Qaeda was led by Osama bin Laden. After he organized the attack on the World Trade Center in 2001, he went into hiding. In 2011, US Special Forces tracked him to a large compound in Abbottabad, Pakistan, where he was killed.

On September 11th, 2001, planes hijacked by al-Qaeda crashed into the World Trade Center in New York, killing some 2,800 people.

AL-QAEDA'S ATTACK

The terrorists did not agree with the way people lived in western society. They believed that everyone in the world should be Muslim and that non-believers were a target for violence. They also thought the United States had too much power in the world, so they attacked the symbols of America's wealth and military power.

After the attacks, US President George W. Bush launched a campaign to strike back at al-Qaeda hideouts in Afghanistan and defeat the Taliban. The United States and Great Britain joined with a group of Afghan warriors called the **Northern Alliance** to fight the Taliban.

George Bush, US President at the time of the September 11th attack.

The Northern Alliance

The local soldiers of the Northern Alliance fought alongside the US and British forces to defeat the Taliban. Without their help, the United States would have needed to send many more soldiers to Afghanistan.

Men from the Taliban Militia (fighting force).

Afghan anti-Taliban fighters take cover when they are fired on by al-Qaeda forces.

⬆ How were the Taliban overthrown?

In October 2001, the United States and Great Britain began bombing Taliban strongholds in Afghanistan. In November, members of the Northern Alliance attacked more outposts, and the Taliban government was overthrown.

Are the Taliban still fighting?

Although they are no longer in government, the Taliban continue to attack Afghan government forces, as well as allied military forces, and lay land mines (bombs underground). They want to retake the country.

The Taliban continue to mount attacks in Afghanistan, hoping to retake power.

WHO RUNS AFGHANISTAN NOW?

Since 2004, the government of Afghanistan has been elected by the people.

It has a president and an elected parliament called the National Assembly. But the country still has many problems. The Taliban attacks are a constant threat, and the Afghan people are extremely poor. Afghanistan needs support from other countries to help it rebuild.

An Afghan Army soldier shows new recruits how to shoot and crawl under fire.

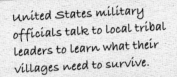

United States military officials talk to local tribal leaders to learn what their villages need to survive.

HELPING OUT

Training Soldiers

The US military are training the soldiers of the Afghan Army, teaching them how to fight in a battle and how to search for land mines, weapons, and Taliban hideouts. The Afghan Army also works to improve living conditions in villages and cities around the country.

Working with Citizens

The United States and its allies (forces fighting alongside) know that to defeat the Taliban, they must be friends with the Afghan people. The best way to do this is to help meet the Afghans' day-to-day needs. They want the Afghans to know that they are not there to take over, but to help give the people a better life.

A military nurse provides medical care to an Afghan child.

What do the Afghan people need?

They need schools and hospitals, since so many have been destroyed during the country's civil wars. Army medical and construction teams are working to provide them.

A British soldier gives out school bags to Afghan children.

How else do the soldiers help out?

The military helps out in schools and hospitals once they are built, providing medical care and equipment.

US soldiers demonstrate how to improve crops.

Why are the soldiers helping the farmers?

If the Afghan farmers can learn better ways to plant crops, they can grow more food and reduce the risk of starvation in Afghanistan.

LEAVING AFGHANISTAN

It may be several more years before foreign troops can bring peace and prosperity to Afghanistan and finally leave the country. The Taliban and other terrorist forces continue to fight for power, and there is a lot of organizing and rebuilding still to do.

ARE ALL THE SOLDIERS FROM THE USA?

The US forces are part of a group called the International Security Assistance Force (ISAF for short).

Troops from different countries work together in the **ISAF** to keep the peace, prevent the Taliban from regaining power, and train the Afghan National Army (ANA) to take on the defense of the country. They are also known as **the coalition forces**.

Who are the coalition forces?

The ISAF is made up of over 130,000 soldiers from around 46 different countries.

They are led by a group called the North Atlantic Treaty Organization (NATO), which consists of 28 North American and European countries. These countries protect and defend each other when needed. After September 11, 2001, NATO joined with the United States to help combat terrorism. In 2003, NATO took on the leadership of the ISAF to fight the terrorists operating in Afghanistan.

ISAF
کمک او همکاری

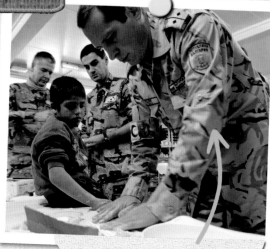

A Bulgarian ISAF armed forces doctor helps an Afghan boy with a broken arm.

A Greek ISAF soldier gives out jackets to children at an orphanage.

A German soldier by an ISAF armored vehicle.

Do the ISAF countries provide equipment?

Many ISAF members have donated war equipment such as ammunition, tanks, rifles, and body armor. They have also brought in supplies for rebuilding projects such as bridges and roads and goods that the Afghan people need such as food, water, medicines, and clothing.

An Italian soldier of the ISAF by relief goods for poor Afghan families.

International troops take cover as they launch an attack on Taliban forces.

Do all the ISAF forces work together?

All the ISAF military forces work together, fighting the Taliban and hunting for land mines. They also work with the local people, helping them to rebuild and govern.

A typical improvised explosive device (IED).

SEARCHING FOR BOMBS

One of the most important jobs the coalition forces do is to search for Improvised Explosive Devices (IEDs for short). These homemade bombs are hidden in buildings and along roads, often injuring innocent people when they explode (find out more on page 12).

11

WHAT JOBS DO THE SOLDIERS DO?

Soldiers in Afghanistan perform lots of different tasks, from fighting the Taliban and hunting for hidden bombs, to helping the local population and rebuilding roads, bridges, and buildings.

The soldiers' training continues even after they come to Afghanistan. They might have to learn new skills to cope with the situations they find, such as dealing with very hot weather or learning to understand the needs of the local people.

Out on patrol

Soldiers go on missions to find and raid Taliban strongholds. Military officers carefully plan these raids so no one gets hurt. Medical helicopters are ready to fly any injured soldiers to the nearest hospital if needed.

Soldiers on patrol must keep an eye out for land mines and snipers (hidden gunmen).

A US Army Explosive Detection Dog and his handler search for land mines. If the dog sniffs explosives, it will let its handler know it has found something suspicious.

DEFUSING BOMBS

Searching for bombs is a job for trained specialist soldiers. They look for wires that may be connected to hidden explosives and use a robot vehicle fitted with cameras to get a closer view. Once the robot finds an IED, it's the soldiers' job to blow it up safely or defuse it. Trained dogs, called Explosive Detection Dogs, are used to sniff out land mines.

How do soldiers stay in touch?

Radio communication is vital, as troops must be in touch with each other to warn of possible Taliban attacks and call in help if they need it. Each soldier carries a personal shortwave radio when out on patrol. Larger communication systems like the radio in the picture (right) allow soldiers to keep in touch over longer distances. The specialist soldiers who look after the equipment must know how it all works and keep it going during sandstorms and freezing weather.

A US Marine Corps field wireman working on communications equipment.

How do soldiers connect the country?

Army engineers build and repair roads so that soldiers can reach military outposts and Afghan people can travel between towns and villages. It's a difficult job because of the weather and the rocky landscape, and the engineers must also watch for bombs and Taliban attacks.

Soldiers examine a road for damage carried out by the Taliban.

BRIDGE-BUILDING

Troops build bridges to make it easier for Afghans to travel and for the Afghan Army to patrol the country. These tough metal bridges should last for 50 years or more.

US Marines build a bridge in Afghanistan.

WHERE DOES EVERYONE LIVE?

The ISAF soldiers live in military camps.

Some of them are massive. The camp at Kandahar is like a small town, with roads, shops, and sports facilities, as well as barracks, canteens, and military buildings.

Large camps such as Kandahar are home to troops from many nations.

Small military outposts in **combat zones** can be much more basic, with a few soldiers living in tents or holes dug into the ground.

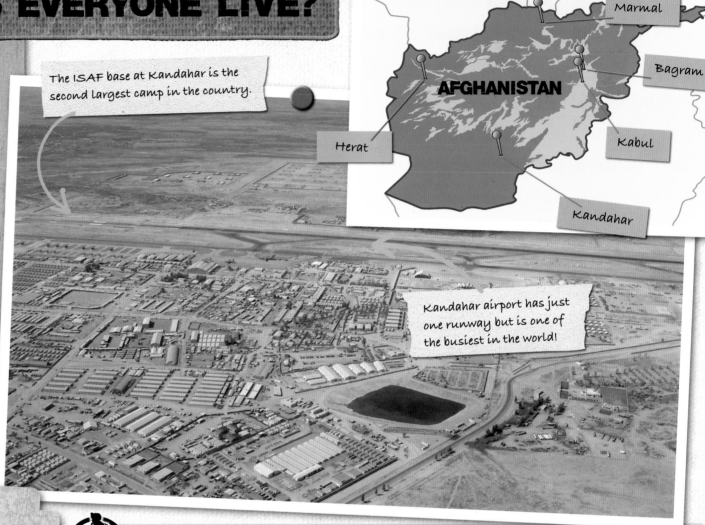

The ISAF base at Kandahar is the second largest camp in the country.

Kandahar airport has just one runway but is one of the busiest in the world!

MAJOR CAMPS IN AFGHANISTAN

AFGHANISTAN

Marmal

Bagram

Herat

Kabul

Kandahar

Military Words

Here are some of the words you might hear in a military camp.

R and R: Rest and Recreation. A chance to take some time off.

Combat zone: An area of the country where fighting is going on.

Insurgents: Enemy forces in Afghanistan.

FOB: Anyone working for the military.

 ## LIFE IN CAMP

Life in camp has its own everyday routines, but personnel must always be alert for the Taliban carrying out ground attacks or firing at them with long-range weapons.

Conditions can be uncomfortable in camp. In the summer, Kandahar is extremely hot and dusty, with temperatures often reaching over 120° Fahrenheit (49° C).

Kandahar Camp Facts

- NATO's largest military base ever.
- Originally built for 12,000, the camp has been expanded to house over 30,000 troops.
- There are 300 aircraft stationed at Kandahar airport, which handles over 5,000 flights each week.
- There's a hockey rink right in the middle of the base.

What do soldiers eat in camp?

Canteens dish out everything from a cooked breakfast to a curry. In many camps, there are even branches of pizza restaurants, burger bars, and coffee shops, just like back home.

The canteens cook and serve thousands of hot meals every day!

Where does everyone sleep?

In camp, the soldiers sleep in purpose-built barracks or tents. It can get pretty cozy, so you have to hope your roommates don't snore.

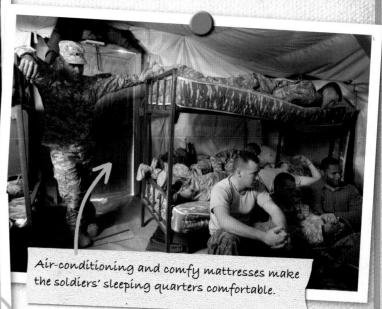

Air-conditioning and comfy mattresses make the soldiers' sleeping quarters comfortable.

Outdoor sports fields are great for playing ball games or frisbee during time off.

What do the soldiers do to relax?

There are lots of ways to relax when you're not on duty. Soldiers keep fit by playing sports or going to the gym. In the larger camps, soldiers can go shopping, or even catch a movie.

How do soldiers keep in touch?

Mail can sometimes take a while to arrive, so many soldiers prefer the phone or the Internet to keep in touch.

It's important for soldiers to be able to keep in touch with loved ones back home.

WHAT IS A DAY ON DUTY LIKE?

Most soldiers will say that each day is different, with its own triumphs and dangers.

Soldiers on patrol start early in the morning searching for Taliban holdouts or land mines. At some point they will stop for food, but they won't end their day until the job is done. They might need to camp far from their main base and might even need to dig a hole to sleep in. They carry all the supplies they need in their backpacks (see page 37).

US Army soldiers returning from a tough day out on patrol

A soldier on patrol in a village field.

 ## A TYPICAL DAY ON PATROL

2:00 a.m. Soldiers march through a muddy field, watching for IEDs.

4:00 a.m. American and ANA (Afghan National Army) soldiers move onto a rooftop in a village where they believe the Taliban are hiding.

Dawn. Soldiers tell the villagers that they will not shoot, unless the Taliban fire first.

9:30 a.m. An Afghan informant leads the soldiers to several IEDs planted in dense undergrowth just outside the village.

10:30 a.m. The Taliban begin firing.

11:00 a.m. Soldiers move to their patrol base in a nearby courtyard. The Taliban continue firing and Americans return their fire. A US soldier is seriously injured in the crossfire and is evacuated to safety.

Midday. Fighting ends and the men find some shade to drink water and eat.

Afternoon to evening. Fighting continues throughout the day.

Nightfall. Eventually it is quiet, but the soldiers know that the next day they will go on searching for the Taliban.

A soldier eating a MRE (Meal-Ready-to-Eat) while out on patrol.

A soldier trains in farming skills that he can pass on to Afghans.

What do soldiers eat on patrol?

If soldiers need to eat out while on patrol, they have MREs (Meals-Ready-to-Eat). Each meal is packed into an aluminum pouch, which can be popped into a type of pack called a "flameless ration heater." A drop of water activates the chemicals in the pack and they heat up, warming up the food in its pouch. Soldiers also have "HOOAH!" energy bars in flavors such as apple and cinnamon, chocolate, peanut butter, or raspberry.

What do soldiers drink on patrol?

It's very important to drink enough water in hot weather. Soldiers on patrol carry water canteens or soft pouches of water with drinking tubes attached, called "hydration packs."

What do other soldiers do?

Not every soldier goes on patrol and for other soldiers, a typical day will be very different. For instance, those who work to help villagers with farming might go to an Afghan village and advise a farmer on his crops or perhaps repair a leaky well. They have very different challenges from the soldiers out on patrol.

A US Marine and an Afghan National Policeman patrol together.

17

WHAT MACHINERY DO SOLDIERS USE?

US and allied forces depend on vehicles, aircraft, and weaponry in their work.

Specialist soldiers repair and maintain the vehicles and aircraft, but all troops learn how to clean and check their own weapons so they are always ready for action.

 ## ON THE ROAD

Humvees

Tough offroad vehicles are best for the rough road conditions of Afghanistan. US military forces use the Humvee, one of the best offroad trucks in the world. It can be fitted with a weapon on the roof, or used as an ambulance, or to transport troops out on patrol.

A Humvee, escorted by two trucks, out on the hunt for IEDs.

Strykers

Armored Stryker vehicles are just one of the armored vehicles used in Afghanistan. They can transport soldiers, carry weapons, or carry out reconnaissance (searching for the enemy). The crew can stay inside for protection from enemy fire.

Stryker Facts

Number of wheels: 8
Engine: Diesel
Top speed: 62 mph
Cost: About $1.42 million

Can be armed with machine guns and a grenade launcher

Air-conditioned

The crew can see out via a periscope

A steel hull and armor-plating to protect from attack

Internal computer screens for tracking friendly forces and enemy movements

Fitted with day-night thermal imaging cameras for seeing in the dark

➲ What is a bomb robot?

Bomb robots are mini remote-controlled vehicles that search for hidden explosives. They can trace an IED and move it off to the side of the road, where a team of soldiers can blow it up or defuse it. Some bomb robots are so small they can be carried in a backpack.

A US Army engineer repairs a remote-controlled bomb robot.

A US soldier on patrol with an M-4 rifle.

 IN THE AIR

US and allied forces use helicopters, fighter jets, aerial refueling planes, transport planes, and **UAVs** in their work. Each type of plane is operated by a different squadron, with their own trained specialists. The squadrons all have nicknames, such as the "Roadrunners" (the Marine Transport Squadron) and the "Watchdogs," "Night Owls," and "Phantoms" (all UVA Squadrons).

Troops on the ground can call in fighter jets to help them fight the enemy.

⬆ What weapons do soldiers carry?

Soldiers on patrol carry an M-4 rifle, a very accurate and fast weapon. They check and clean their gun every day, separating all the parts and dusting them with a brush or a rag.

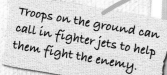

What is a UAV?

A UAV (unmanned aerial vehicle) is a pilotless plane that can be operated from far away, by computer. US forces use them for reconnaissance or arm them to attack enemy targets. Onboard radar and video cameras transmit information back to the operators on the ground. They're also called "drones."

A US Marine launches a surveillance UAV to track Taliban movements in the countryside.

WHAT'S IT LIKE ON A BASE BACK HOME?

Soldiers' families live back home on US military bases.

They get emails and phone messages from their loved ones in action abroad, but they sometimes need help to handle the problems of daily life.

HELPING THE CHILDREN WHO "SERVE"

In many ways, the children of military families are helping their country, too. They have to cope with their loved ones being away, stay strong, and help the family they live with back home.

Sometimes the military forces organize special day camps for these children, where they can have fun and meet other children like themselves. Entertainers sometimes come and present shows for them to give them a treat.

A little boy whose parent is serving abroad at a day event designed to help him understand what life is like on duty.

Kids learning to salute at a day camp run by the Army.

Santa Claus pays a visit to an Air Force base.

An entertainer reads a book to children at a military base.

Do families chat?

Some websites host chat rooms for soldiers' families so they can talk about their problems or share their thoughts. It's also a good way to meet new friends in a similar position. There is more about how military families feel on page 42.

The Internet helps families to stay in touch with one another.

Who visits?

Sometimes military bases at home and abroad get important visitors. They may be US politicians or entertainers who want to show their support for the efforts that the soldiers and their families are making for their country.

US President Barack Obama and the First Lady Michelle Obama drop in on a US military base.

When do soldiers come home?

The best part of having a family member in the military is the day he or she comes home. Soldiers get regular leave (time off) from their duties and fly home to see their families for a while.

US Navy pilots come home after completing a tour onboard an aircraft carrier.

HOW HAS THE WAR CHANGED LIVES?

Some Afghan people have seen improvement in their lives, but others have lost their homes and jobs and live in refugee camps.

During the fighting, many villagers fled their homes and went to the capital, Kabul. Others moved to Pakistan in 2001, then returned to Afghanistan when they thought it was safe. But they found they had nowhere to live and no jobs when they returned.

Afghan children cannot remember a time when their country was at peace. Thousands are orphaned, homeless, and very poor. But for some children, life has gotten better, and they can now go to school and get medical care.

GOING TO SCHOOL

When the Taliban ruled, girls were not allowed to go to school or college. Now many girls attend school regularly. It's estimated that 52% of Afghan men and 22% of women can read and write. Since the war, international charities such as the United Nations Children's Fund (UNICEF) have set up schools around the country.

An Afghan girl doing her schoolwork. Girls are no longer banned from attending school.

> **Now I can read the first volume textbook and write.**
>
> An Afghan teenage girl, finally able to attend school.

What is a refugee camp?

When there is fighting in an area, the people who live there might have to leave because their homes have been destroyed and their lives put in danger. These people are called refugees and often move to makeshift camps, where they rely on charities to help them to survive.

A sandstorm blows through a refugee camp in Kabul.

What is it like living in a refugee camp?

Refugee camps are very tough places to live. Homes are often makeshift tents, which can leak when it rains. Many of the refugees have lost loved ones in the fighting and have no way of making a living. Afghan camps are often Taliban recruiting grounds, where the terrorists get people to join them by promising them a better life.

Children play football in front of bombed-out ruins in Kabul. Many people lost their homes during the fighting.

> **War has affected us in a way that makes life horrible. We have lost our parents.**
>
> An Afghan boy in a war-torn village.

What is being done to help refugees?

International organizations such as UNICEF and the World Food Program are working to improve conditions in Afghanistan's refugee camps, providing food, shelter, and education. The United States has contributed over $700 million in aid to help the effort.

Children line up to get food given out by UNICEF at a refugee camp.

23

WHERE IS IRAQ?

Iraq, a country in the Middle East, is home to 31 million people.

Its capital is Baghdad, and it has two main rivers, the Tigris and the Euphrates. Most of Iraq is flat, with desert and broad river valleys. The northeast is more mountainous. The desert regions are very hot in summer, but up in the mountains it is cooler, with winter snow.

Once called Mesopotamia, Iraq is a historic region that has some of the oldest archaeological remains in the world.

IRAQ IN THE WORLD

TURKEY

SYRIA

Dahuk

Al Mawsil

Arbil

Karkuk

As Sulaymaniyah

IRAN

KEY
- Desert
- Non desert
- Mountains

Samarra

Ar Ramadi

BAGHDAD

IRAQ

Karbala

Al Hillah

Al Kut

Ad Diwaniyah

An Najaf

River Tigris

River Euphrates

An Nasiriyah

Al Basrah

N
W — E
S

CANADA

UNITED KINGDOM

RUSSIA

UNITED STATES

CHINA

United States

SAHARA

BRAZIL

Iraq

AUSTRALIA

The remains of palaces and temples, such as these in the ancient city of Hatra, are a reminder of Iraq's historic past.

RELIGION IN IRAQ

Islam is the country's main religion, but its followers are divided into two different groups called the Sunni Muslims and the Shi'ite (Shia) Muslims. The holy book of the Islamic religion is the Koran. Its teachings are followed by Muslims and include praying five times a day in the direction of the holy city of Mecca in Saudi Arabia.

Marshlands in the south and east of Iraq are home to tribes known as the Marsh Arabs, who farm and fish.

What do people do in Iraq?

In Iraq's cities there are many businesses selling food, clothing, and goods of all descriptions. In the countryside, people live in small villages, farming crops and animals. Wages in Iraq are very low compared to those of the rest of the world, and many people do not have enough food to eat.

The Koran sets out the rules of the Muslim religion, which are followed by most people in Iraq.

IRAQI OIL

Iraq has huge oil reserves (oil stored underground). That makes it very important to the rest of the world because its oil is vital for fueling industry and transport in other countries.

The Baiji oil refinery, north of Baghdad.

WHAT LED TO WAR?

Saddam Hussein, a Sunni Muslim, became President of Iraq in 1979 and ruled with the help of the Iraqi military.

Groups that opposed Saddam, such as the Shi'ite Muslims and the Kurds, became victims of murder and torture.

In September 1980, Saddam Hussein attacked neighboring Iran, which was controlled by radical Shi'ite Muslims. The US supported Iraq in this war because of Iran's support for anti-American terrorists.

A COSTLY WAR

Invasion of Kuwait

The Iran-Iraq war was very expensive for Saddam Hussein, costing Iraq around $120 billion. Meanwhile, huge oil reserves had been discovered in neighboring Kuwait, making it a very rich country. It had once been a part of Iraq, so Saddam wanted to grab it back.

Saddam claimed Kuwait should still be part of Iraq and invaded it to "reclaim" its vast oil wealth, despite objections by other countries. Saddam also used chemical weapons (poison gas) to kill rebellious Iraqi Kurds in the northern part of his own country.

Under the leadership of Saddam Hussein, Iraq attacked its neighbors, Iran and Kuwait.

US troops during "Operation Desert Storm."

DESERT STORM

In response, the United States formed a coalition with Saudi Arabia, the U.K., and other western countries and attacked Iraq on January 17, 1991. The action was called Operation Desert Storm and drove Saddam's armies out of Kuwait.

US soldiers in an armored vehicle during the invasion of Iraq in 2003.

Weapons inspectors were sent to Iraq to find evidence of nuclear and chemical weapons.

⬅ What are WMDs?

Weapons of mass destruction are often called "WMDs" for short. These are weapons that can kill many people at once, such as nuclear or chemical bombs. Saddam Hussein was thought to be hiding them in Iraq, ready for use. He continually refused to allow UN weapons inspectors to look for evidence that Iraq had WMDs.

⬆ Why did coalition forces attack Iraq again?

On September 11, 2001, the New York World Trade Center Towers were destroyed by terrorists (see page 6). President Bush decided Saddam Hussein was supporting the forces that planned the attack. He also became convinced that Iraq was developing weapons of mass destruction (WMDs), so the United States declared war on Iraq in 2003.

Baghdad was heavily bombed during the invasion in 2003.

DID EVERYONE AGREE WITH THE WAR?

Many world nations wanted to hold further talks with Iraq and cut off its trade rather than invade the country.

On November 8, 2002, the **United Nations Security Council** blamed Iraq for not allowing international weapons inspection teams to look for hidden weapons but did not agree to declaring war.

The United States and the U.K. decided to go ahead and remove Saddam Hussein's government by force, though many people around the world did not agree and protested against the invasion.

> "France is not anti-American... But we just feel that there is another option... than war."
>
> French president Jacques Chirac speaks against the war.

> "A free Iraq... will be a decisive blow to terrorism ... and a victory for the security of America and the civilized world.
>
> US President George Bush speaks to the United Nations.

What is the United Nations Security Council?

The Security Council is a part of the United Nations, an organization in which the world's nations get together to discuss important issues. The Security Council tries to maintain international peace and security. It has five permanent members—China, France, the United Kingdom, the United States, and Russia. Other countries take turns participating in the Council.

There were demonstrations against the war in many European countries. Here protestors march through Berlin, Germany.

The United Nations Security Council meeting in New York in 2003, to discuss Iraq.

28

What finally started the war?

The United States and its allies decided that Saddam Hussein was capable of carrying out great violence. They thought that if he really did have WMDs, he might soon attack his neighbors. His army had already used poison gas to attack his opponents in his own country. So, on March 18, 2003, war began against Iraq.

Smoke rises from a building at a popular market in Baghdad in 2007. This bomb attack killed 65 people.

US troops use night vision equipment like the device mounted on this soldier's helmet to spot enemies in the dark.

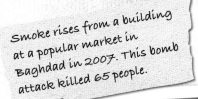

⬅ How did the Iraq war end?

The United States and its allies swept into Baghdad and began an occupation (rule). Saddam Hussein was captured and hanged after a trial in an Iraqi court found him guilty of terrible crimes against the Iraqi people. Some believe he gave support to the al-Qaeda terrorists who conducted the 2001 attack on New York, though a direct connection has never been proved. Weapons of mass destruction were never discovered.

⬅ Why are coalition troops still there?

Enemies of the US and coalition troops formed bands of armed fighters called insurgents. Since the war ended, there have been many insurgent attacks on military and civilian targets. The coalition forces have stayed to try to stop these insurgents from taking over the country while the people of Iraq settle on a new form of government.

WHY IS THERE STILL FIGHTING IN IRAQ?

There are a number of different reasons why people are still fighting in Iraq.

Some Iraqis are fighting the coalition forces because they feel they were forced into having a government they didn't agree with. Some fight for religious reasons and others because of long-running disputes between tribal or religious groups within Iraq.

 ## LOCAL FIGHTING FORCES

Al-Qaeda

Many attacks are organized by al-Qaeda, an international terrorist group. Their aim is to upset the economies and influence of Western nations to further their extremist religious aims. You can find out more about them on page 6.

Abu Musab al-Zarqawi, an al-Qaeda leader in Iraq. He was killed in an air raid in 2006.

Members of the Iraqi Army being trained by US and coalition forces to take over security in Iraq.

The Iraqi Army

The Iraqi Army is now being trained by US and coalition forces so that they can take over the defense of their country when foreign troops finally leave.

Warlords

Warlords are armed chieftains who hold power in local regions and are often involved in regional fighting. They control the people in their area and command their own fighting men. Both the terrorists and coalition forces want their loyalty.

➲ Who are the victims of terrorist violence?

Besides soldiers, large numbers of innocent Iraqi people have been killed by car bombs and suicide bombers. Busy places such as town markets are often targeted. In addition, local officials such as politicians have sometimes been killed or kidnapped.

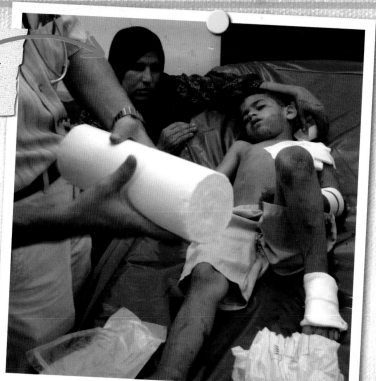

An Iraqi boy wounded by a suicide bomb attack, which took place during a funeral in 2008.

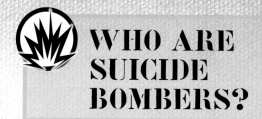

WHO ARE SUICIDE BOMBERS?

Insurgents with extreme religious beliefs are convinced that a beautiful life after death awaits anyone who kills those with a different point of view. Some individuals are persuaded to become suicide bombers, blowing themselves and others up in surprise attacks.

THE IRAQI POLICE

The Iraqi Police help protect businesses and homes from crime, and they help man checkpoints, too. Iraqi cities have many checkpoints in their streets, places where cars and trucks are stopped and searched for bombs and terrorists.

Cadets from the Iraqi Police Academy parade during their graduation ceremony in 2011.

HOW IS IRAQ RUN TODAY?

In 2005, elections were held in Iraq for the first time to create a government to pass laws and restore the country to normal life.

The government is led by a Prime Minister, under a President who is elected every four years by the members of the government. The Iraqis voted on **Election Day**.

What is Election Day?

Election Day is a day when people vote for whom they want to form a government and run their country. In Iraq, each voter had his or her finger dabbed with blue dye so no one could vote more than once. The voters were very proud of their blue fingers, because it showed they had taken part.

These Muslim women are from the Shi'ite religious group, which has the most power in government.

Iraqi lawmakers gather in the Iraqi Parliament in Baghdad.

A Sunni Muslim man celebrates following a local Iraqi election. The Sunni religious group are part of the government.

Voters proudly show their inky fingers, proof that they voted in Iraq's first democratic election in 2005.

MAIN GOVERNMENT GROUPS

There are two main Muslim religious groups in the government, the Shi'ites and the Sunni. The Shi'ites are in the majority (have the most members) and the Sunni are in the minority (have fewer members).

Both groups are Muslim, but they have political differences that began back in history, in the time after the death of the Prophet Muhammad. Shi'ite Muslims wanted future religious and political leaders to be descendants of Muhammad's cousin and son-in-law. The Sunni Muslims wanted the leaders to be elected from Muhammad's followers.

Saddam Hussein's followers were mostly Sunni Muslims. After the war, the Shi'ites came into power.

Iraqi religious groups have their own places of worship. The Great Mosque of Samarra is a religious center for Shi'ites.

Christians:
Besides Muslims, there are roughly 1.5 million Christians in Iraq, who form various different Christian groups.

Turkmen:
Turkmen live in the north and are mostly Sunni Muslims whose ancestors were invaders from central Asia.

Yezidi:
Kurdish people follow Yezidi beliefs that combine Muslim beliefs with the ancient teachings of the Zoroastrian religion.

Mandaeans:
About 50,000 Mandaeans combine ancient beliefs with the teachings of John the Baptist. Their holy book is called the Ginza Rba.

Is the government working?

Al-Qaeda terrorists and tribal warlords continue to mount attacks, but constant patrols have made it harder for terrorists to succeed. As life has improved in the country, fewer people want to join them. Now foreign countries are "drawing down" (removing their troops) from Iraq and turning over the security to trained Iraqi soldiers.

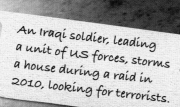

An Iraqi soldier, leading a unit of US forces, storms a house during a raid in 2010, looking for terrorists.

WHAT JOBS DO SOLDIERS DO IN IRAQ?

In Iraq today, American and coalition forces help to patrol and rebuild.

Soldiers patrol possible terrorist trouble spots, trying to prevent suicide bomb attacks and ambushes, and looking for **IEDs** to defuse. Soldiers also work with the Iraqi people to rebuild the country after years of war.

More about IEDs

IED stands for "Improvised Explosive Device." Terrorists build IEDs from explosive material such as artillery shells or C-4, which looks like modeling clay. The explosive is connected to an electric device such as a cell phone that can be triggered from a distance by dialing its number. Highly-trained Army experts do the dangerous work of defusing the bombs.

> "I don't want my nephews fighting a fight I couldn't finish. I want them to go to college, or play professional soccer, or be beach bums. However, if they choose to become soldiers I would be proud to be in the same chain that links all military personnel, past and present, the chain that holds America together."
>
> American soldier's blog—Iraq.

A US Navy specialist builder working in a Naval Mobile Construction Team, repairing a damaged building.

⬆ What do soldier specialists do?

Soldier specialists work with Iraqis building homes, schools, and hospitals, and repairing services such as water, electricity, and roads. They've also helped rebuild and guard oil platforms and equipment. Iraq's oil trade is very important because it earns vital money for the country.

A British Army specialist dog handler trains his dog to search for IEDs (find out more about mine dogs on page 12).

How else do soldiers help out?

Sometimes soldiers put down their weapons and pitch in to help take much-needed goods such as food, bottled drinking water, and medical supplies to important locations such as hospitals.

Iraqi Police watch US soldiers enter a building to look for terrorist suspects.

A US Marine talks to Iraqi children during an operation to bring medical care and supplies to their home area.

How do troops work with the police?

Troops help the Iraqi Police to patrol neighborhoods and man checkpoints in cities and towns. It makes daily life much easier if people can be confident that they will not be attacked.

What are anti-terrorist patrols?

US and coalition forces patrol in armored vehicles, especially in places where there are reports of terrorist activity. Iraqi Army soldiers usually come along on the patrols and will eventually take over all anti-terrorist duties.

US Army troops out on patrol, returning to their armored vehicle after searching a bridge for IEDs.

WHAT DO SOLDIERS WEAR?

A soldier's clothes must be comfortable and practical in different situations.

Soldiers from different countries wear different types of uniforms with different insignia (badges) on them. US Army troops wear ACUs (Army Combat Uniform) in camouflage colors.

TAGS AND PATCHES

The soldiers' jackets are marked with insignia such as stripes that indicate their rank and badges that represent the part of the army they belong to. On each arm they have an IR IFF tag, an infrared "identify friendly forces" marking. This tag shows up when seen through night vision equipment, making it easier for soldiers to identify friendly troops in the dark.

A soldier with an arm patch on his uniform.

HEADGEAR

Out on combat operations soldiers wear a MICH helmet. MICH stands for "modular integrated communications helmet."

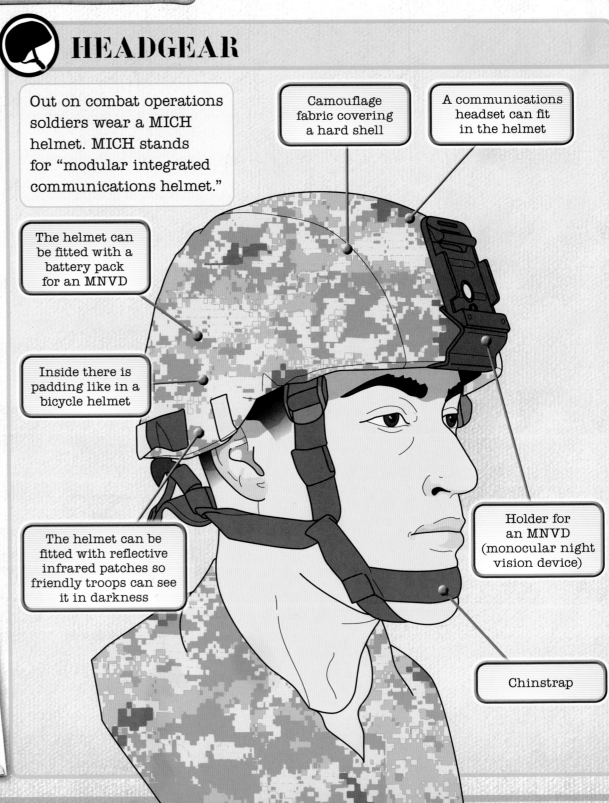

Camouflage fabric covering a hard shell

A communications headset can fit in the helmet

The helmet can be fitted with a battery pack for an MNVD

Inside there is padding like in a bicycle helmet

The helmet can be fitted with reflective infrared patches so friendly troops can see it in darkness

Holder for an MNVD (monocular night vision device)

Chinstrap

CLOTHING ON PATROL

Here is a typical Army Combat Uniform worn out on patrol.

Camouflage without the color black in it, because black shows up too much when seen through night vision equipment

The pattern of the desert camouflage uniform is made up of all the colors found in the desert to help soldiers blend into their surroundings—making it hard for the enemy to spot them.

T-shirt made of fabric that is good at "wicking," allowing sweat to pass through it and out into the air

Socks made of "wicking" fabric

Tough leather combat boots the color of sand

Backpack weighing between 40 and 60 lbs. for extra equipment, needed if staying away from a base

M-4 rifle

Kevlar™ body armor—a wrap-around bullet-proof vest that weighs around 30lb. Kevlar™ is a type of material that is light but incredibly strong.

Flame-resistant trousers and jacket with useful pockets

A soldier's patrol equipment includes a weapon such as a rifle.

A soldier fires his M-4 weapon during a live firing exercise in Kuwait

⬆ What else does a soldier carry?

As well as a rifle or machine gun, soldiers carry extra ammunition and a first aid kit. They might have grenades, 9mm pistols, night-vision gun sights, and radio communications equipment.

WHAT DO MILITARY MEDICAL TEAMS DO?

US and coalition soldiers receive the finest medical care from trained military personnel.

Portable hospitals are set up close to combat areas for fast treatment, and back at the main bases there are larger hospitals with more equipment and staff.

What do the FSTs have to help them?

FSTs have lots of vital medical machinery, such as mini scanning machines and monitors, oxygen supplies, blood transfusion materials, surgical equipment, and roll-up stretchers. They're able to treat as many as 30 wounded soldiers at a time.

Tents fitted together to create a makeshift hospital.

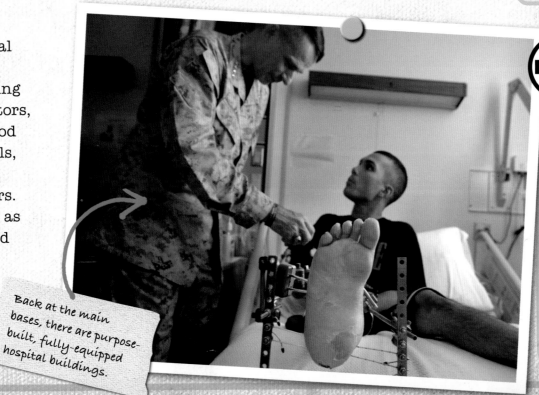

Back at the main bases, there are purpose-built, fully-equipped hospital buildings.

HELP COMES FAST

Fast-moving mobile medical teams called "FSTs" (Forward Surgical Teams) operate behind the troops in combat. They travel in Humvee vehicles and can set up a working mini-hospital with beds, medical equipment, and operating tables in an incredible 60 minutes. They use Deployable Rapid Assembly Shelter ("drash") tents that form a makeshift hospital building.

✚ HOSPITALS BACK HOME

Wounded soldiers go back to large base hospitals, where they can recover over time and get any specialist care they need. Some are sent back to their home countries to recover, accompanied on the way by medical teams.

What other work do doctors do?

Military doctors and nurses don't just treat battle wounds. A lot of their work is treating illnesses that anyone might get, such as stomach ache or toothache. They work alongside Iraqi doctors and nurses treating local people, too.

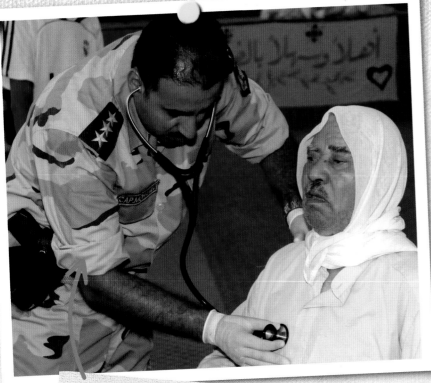

An Iraqi Army surgeon checks the health of a local patient.

> **I think it's important ...I know we learn a lot from each other.**
>
> A US military nurse describes working closely with Iraqi medical staff.

What is "rapid evacuation"?

Troops can use their radios to call in medical help for "rapid evacuation"—taking wounded soldiers quickly away from the combat zone and back to a hospital.

Specially-adapted "medevac" helicopters fly in to pick up the wounded. Onboard the helicopter, medical staff care for the injured on the way to a field hospital.

Troops carry a wounded soldier to a "medevac" helicopter.

HOW DO WE KNOW WHAT'S HAPPENING IN IRAQ?

News footage about the conflict in Iraq often appears on TV and online.

This information is gathered by journalists and camera teams around the country. Since 2003, reporters and photographers have been **"embedded"** with fighting units.

What does "embedded" mean?

Embedded reporters and photographers accompany fighting units and report on their work. If they want to be embedded, they must sign a contract agreeing not to report anything that endangers the war effort, such as giving away military secrets or damaging the morale (mental wellbeing) of the soldiers.

A cameraman films a soldier at work at a checkpoint.

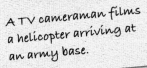

A TV cameraman films a helicopter arriving at an army base.

GATHERING NEWS

TV reporters work alongside a camera operator and a sound recordist, so they can show the scene and broadcast sounds as well as describe it in words. The news teams might ride aboard armored vehicles with daily patrols or fly to distant parts of the country to report on the conflict there.

How does the news travel from Iraq?

Journalists send their stories and pictures to magazines, newspapers, and websites using computers and "uplinks" that transmit the material up to communication satellites orbiting in space. The satellites send the material back to another world location via a "downlink."

A TV news team runs for safety during fighting in Baghdad in 2003.

Reporters and photographers wear bullet-proof vests, just as soldiers do.

Do journalists face danger?

Journalists are exposed to the same dangers as the soldiers they follow. Sadly, a number of news media workers have lost their lives in Iraq. The local people who help them, such as their drivers and interpreters, have also suffered casualties.

HOW DO FAMILIES BACK HOME FEEL?

It's difficult for anyone to have a family member deployed to a dangerous combat area in a country far away.

Each night on TV, there are TV stories about the war, sometimes about soldiers being killed. So how do families feel, and how do they cope?

On large bases, soldiers can stay in touch with home via the Internet.

Getting a letter from home is always a special event for any soldier abroad.

← Do soldiers contact their families back home?

Soldiers can talk to their families, and get letters and presents from them. In the main military bases they can use computers to email their loved ones and get messages from them, too.

Military families can meet up with each other and get help with problems.

"We miss Daddy when he goes away ...When he's here we play video games together, and he takes me places. I want him to get home."

A six-year-old girl who lives with her family on a military base in the United States.

JOINING TOGETHER

In towns and military bases, families of soldiers find it helps to meet with other families who have the same problems as them, such as missing their loved ones or worrying about the fighting.

Do coalition soldiers' kids think about Iraqi kids?

Many children see Iraqi and Afghan youngsters on television and wonder how their families get by and if they can go to school. Do they worry about bombs and bullets, for instance?

Many children are affected by the war, both in the Middle East and in coalition countries.

What's it like when a soldier comes home?

When soldiers come home, it can be difficult for them to overcome the stress of the daily dangers they faced. They might jump at loud noises and have bad dreams, for instance. Meanwhile, family members might have missed them so much, they don't want to leave them for a moment! These feelings are understandable, and families get advice about them.

A Navy officer hugs his daughters before going aboard his ship for another tour of duty.

45

WHAT IS LIFE LIKE FOR CHILDREN IN IRAQ?

Children are the innocent victims in every war.

In Iraq, many years of civil war, as well as the latest troubles, have affected their daily lives.

A number of Iraqi children still live in refugee camps, and their families sometimes struggle to find food and work. Some refugee children have found new lives in countries away from Iraq.

⟵ How does war affect children?

Living through explosions, fire, and the deaths of friends and neighbors is very frightening. Those who experience it often find it hard to cope with what has happened to them. It can affect how they feel throughout their lives.

A young Iraqi girl peers out of the gate as US soldiers go by.

Refugee children living in a camp, having lost their homes.

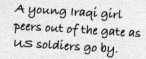

> **We were in the refugee camp for four years. That was my life—the tents, the dirt, and all the people around. I remember being scared every night.**

A boy interviewed about his life in a refugee camp.

44

⬅ Are Iraqi children scared of US troops?

Iraqi children were frightened of the foreign troops who arrived in their country. It was natural for them to feel that way. The coalition soldiers try hard to work with local children to make them feel less anxious.

A boy going home with useful items such as a lamp and cooking pots, given by an aid agency.

US and coalition soldiers work with local children. Here children are taking part in games and finding out how to look after their teeth.

Despite the devastation, many children are still positive about the future.

AID AGENCIES IN IRAQ

Many aid agencies are working in Iraq to supply food, housing, medical care, and education to the people. There is more about the work of international charities on page 22.

45

GLOSSARY

ACU: Initials standing for "Army Combat Uniform," worn by US soldiers

AID AGENCY: A charity organization that gives help to local people, such as food, medical care, and schooling

AL-QAEDA: An Arab terrorist group that believes in using violence to overthrow those who do not follow their religious and political beliefs

ALLY: A country that gives help and support to another

BODY ARMOR: A bullet-proof padded vest made of very tough material, worn by soldiers out on patrol

BOMB ROBOT: A remote-controlled vehicle that can find and move a bomb

CIVIL WAR: Fighting between different groups of people belonging to one country

COALITION FORCES: Troops from the US and other countries fighting alongside each other in Afghanistan and Iraq

COMBAT ZONE: An area where fighting is going on

ELECTIONS: When people vote to choose who governs their country

EMBEDDED: When journalists and camera crews go along with soldiers and report on their work

FST: FST stands for "Forward Surgical Team," mobile hospital units that set up near areas of fighting

HUMVEE: An off-road truck used by the US Army

IED: Initials short for "improvised explosive device," meaning a homemade bomb

INSIGNIA: Badges worn by members of the armed forces to show their rank or the group they belong to

INSURGENT: A fighter who keeps his or her identity hidden and blends in with local people to escape capture

ISAF: The International Security Assistance Force, troops from different countries working together to prevent the Taliban returning to power in Afghanistan

ISLAM: The religion of the followers of the Prophet Muhammad. Most people in Afghanistan and Iraq follow the religion of Islam.

KORAN: The Holy Book of Islam

KURDISH PEOPLE: A group of people who live in the Middle East, in areas of Iran, Syria, Iraq, and Turkey

LAND MINE: A bomb buried in the ground

MEDEVAC HELICOPTER: A helicopter fitted with medical equipment, for transporting wounded soldiers

MICH HELMET: A type of helmet worn by soldiers out on patrol. The initials stand for "modular integrated communications helmet."

MUSLIM: A follower of the religion of Islam

NATO: The North Atlantic Treaty Organization, a group of 28 North American and European countries who work together to protect and defend one another

NATIONAL ASSEMBLY: The elected Parliament of Afghanistan

NORTHERN ALLIANCE: A group of Afghan fighters who oppose the Taliban

NUCLEAR MISSILE: A type of weapon capable of killing many people

RAPID EVACUATION: Taking wounded soldiers quickly away from combat zones and off to the hospital

REFUGEE CAMP: A settlement of temporary homes, such as tents, giving shelter to people made homeless by war

SNIPER: A lone, hidden gunman

STRYKER: An eight-wheeled armored vehicle used by the US Army

SUICIDE BOMBER: Someone who blows themselves up to cause death and destruction

TALIBAN: A group who ruled Afghanistan in the 1990s and have been fighting to retake the country

TERRORIST: Someone who mounts surprise attacks on people or places for the purposes of creating fear and panic as well as death

UAV: Initials that stand for "unmanned aerial vehicle," a remote-controlled pilotless aircraft, also called a "drone"

UNITED NATIONS: An organization in which nations of the world gather together to discuss important issues

WARLORD: An armed chieftain who holds power in a local area

WMDs: Initials short for "weapons of mass destruction," meaning weapons capable of killing very many people at once, such as nuclear bombs